DEDICATION

This book is dedicated to Piikani Nation community, in hope for a brighter future.

The publication and printing of this book is made possible through funding provided by Indigenous & Community Connections/Alberta Advanced Education.

Pincher Creek Community Adult Learning Program would like to thank our funders, partners, learners and staff for their passion and belief in this project.

ACKNOWLEDGMENTS

Dolly Yellow Wings – Illustrator

Emma Lee Warrior – Blackfoot Linguistic Translator

Lucille Provost – Writer

Pat Yellow Wings	Joey Holloway
Bernadette Striped Squirrel	Wesley Scott
Lori Good Rider	Kendall White Cow
Claudia Wolf Tail	Robert Provost
Carmen Prest	Terry Small Legs
Leona English	Cheyenne Crazy Boy
Neena Yellow Face	Danielle One Owl
Ashley North Peigan	Jewel Provost
Marilyn Prairie Chicken	Serena Big Bull
Blair Yellow Wings	Jenny Yellow Horn
Ayesha Yellow Face	Neil Sharp Adze
Diana North Peigan	Tanis Smith
Evan North Peigan	Calvin Prairie Chicken
Dallas Prairie Chicken	Daniel Woody Northman
Herman Many Guns	

FORWARD

The intention of this book is to replant seeds of hope for the power of having dreams and becoming empowered to achieve them.

This book is written by the people of Piikani, for the people of Piikani. Thank you for your bravery and for inspiring those around you.

IF I COULD DREAM FOR PIIKANI TODAY ...

COPYRIGHT 2018   © Pincher Creek CALP
ISBN: 978-1721953684

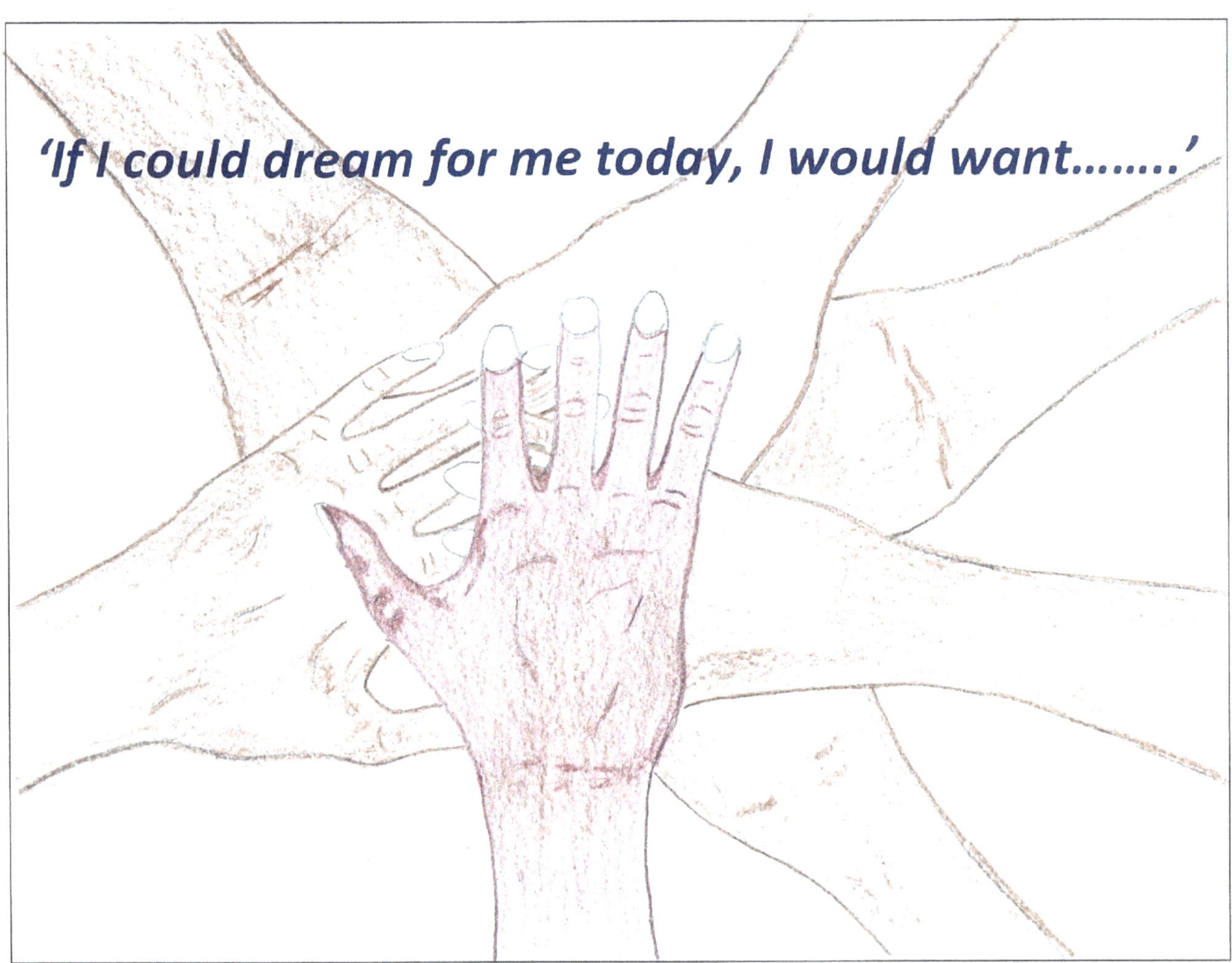
'If I could dream for me today, I would want……..'

To all be treated equally

Ah kaoh ka nai to ma ni to totsp

'If I could dream for me today, I would want........'
Git-skin, neep?
ah...

Piikani people to all speak Blackfoot Language

Piikani mahkaitsipois

‘If I could dream for me today, I would want……..’

For children to learn native dancing,
that I teach them dancing

Pokaiks mahkaipaiskahsa Ahkitstsisi matapi
mahkaisksinimatsahsaiks

'If I could dream for me today, I would want........'

Peigans to be on good terms with fellow Peigans

Piikanitapiiks mahkai soksi ksoko wam otsiisa

'If I could dream for me today, I would want........'

Piikani to heal the past hurts

Pikaniitapi mahk sokinohsa

'If I could dream for me today, I would want........'

That I appreciate life

Nitahkaiksimatsitsis patapiisin

'If I could dream for me today, I would want……..'

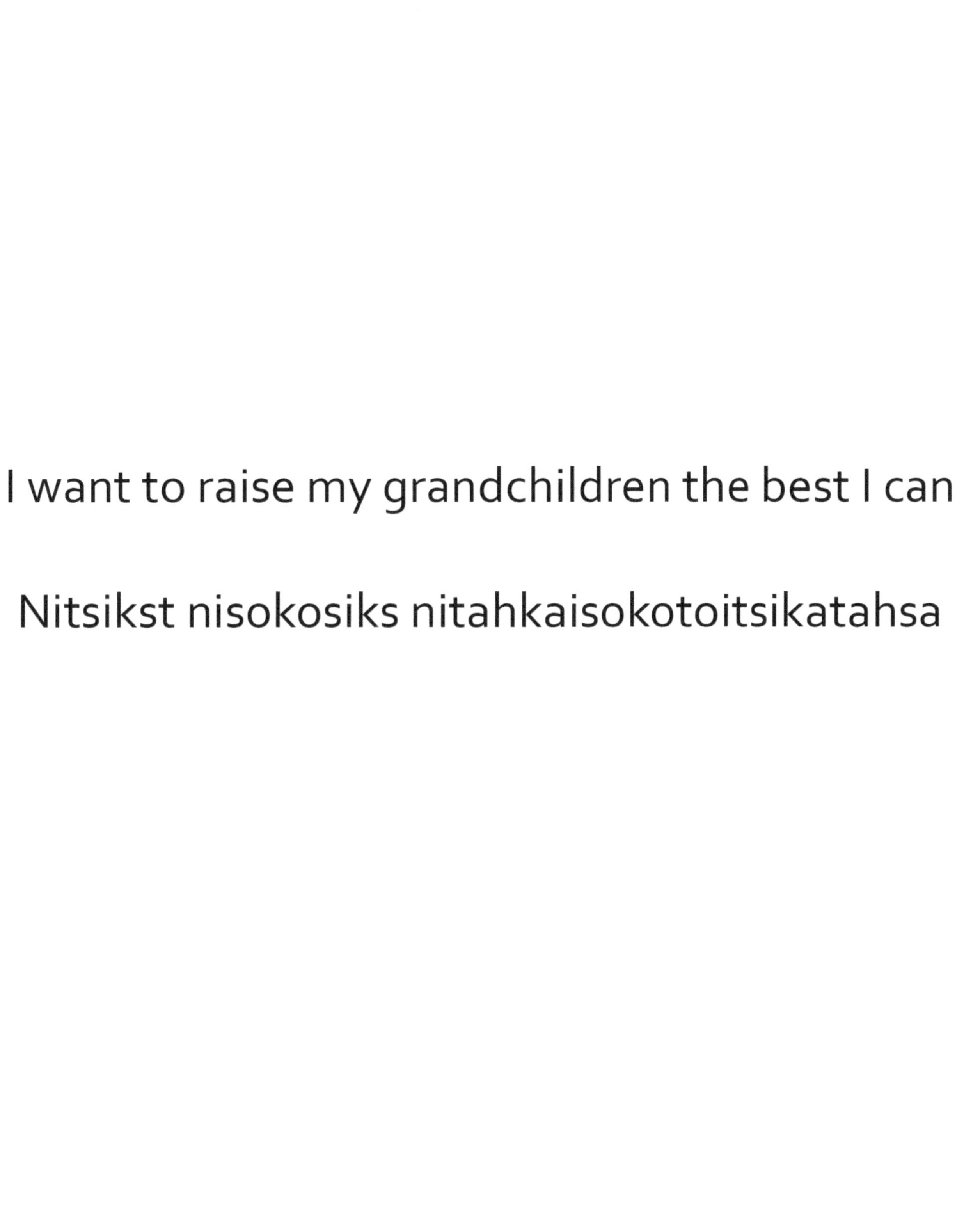

I want to raise my grandchildren the best I can

Nitsikst nisokosiks nitahkaisokotoitsikatahsa

'If I could dream for me today, I would want........'
Piikani Vet Clinic
OPEN

To provide health care for my pets

Nitahkaisokinahsi nitskanitamiks

'If I could dream for me today, I would want……..'

Everyone to be educated

Ahkohkanai ispsksinimatsahs matapiwa

'If I could dream for me today, I would want........'

Old people to be included in teaching children

Omahkitapiiks mahkaisksinimatstohksa

Bank of Piikani Nation
'If I could dream for me today, I would want........'
Piikani Grocery Store
Piikani Hardware Store
ESSO
Piikani Pawn

We Peigans to have service stations, grocery stores and a bank

Kistonon Piikaniwa ahkainaniosi itawahkittop, itowahsohpomopi, itayakihtop intaohpomopi

'If I could dream for me today, I would want........'

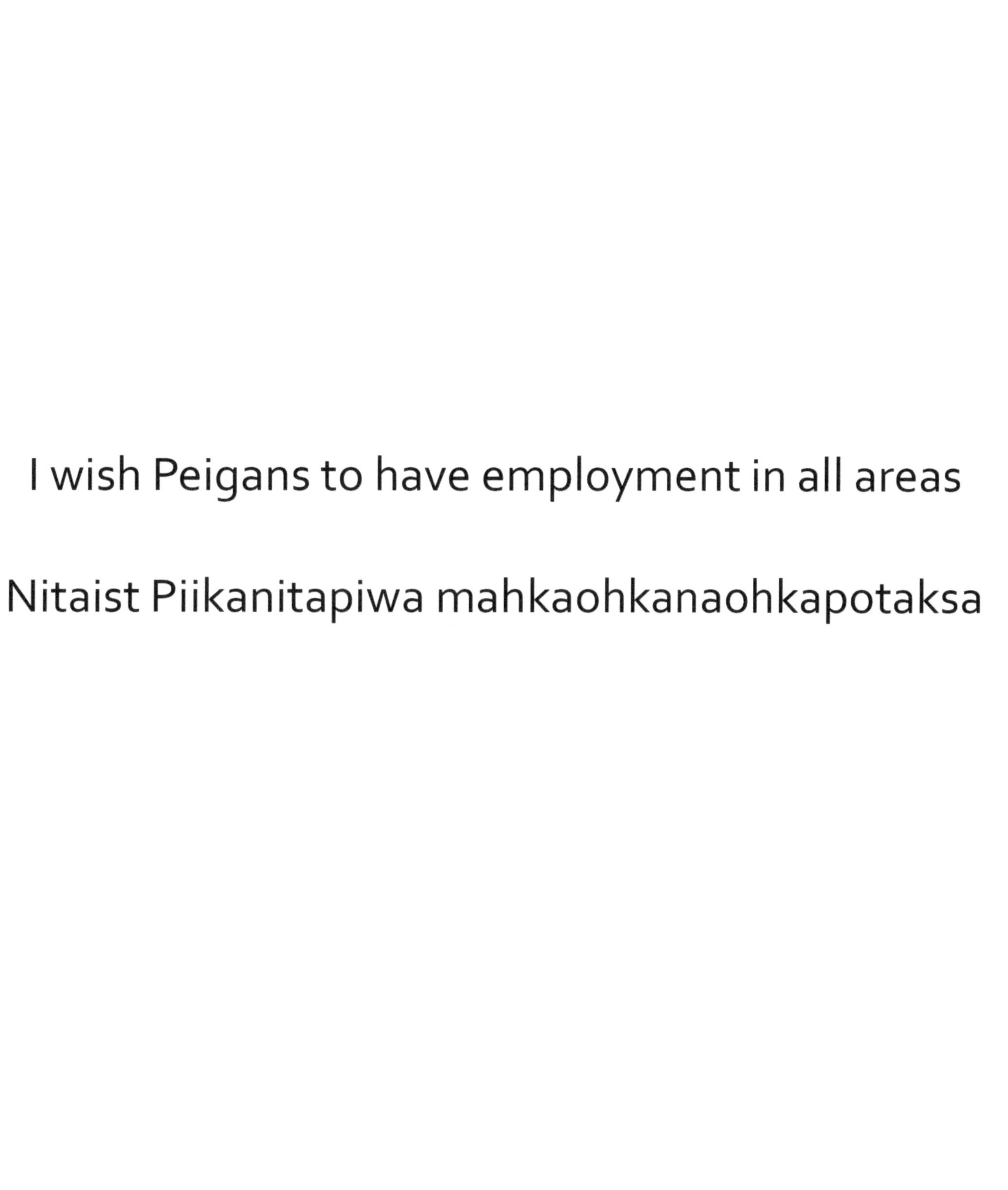

I wish Peigans to have employment in all areas

Nitaist Piikanitapiwa mahkaohkanaohkapotaksa

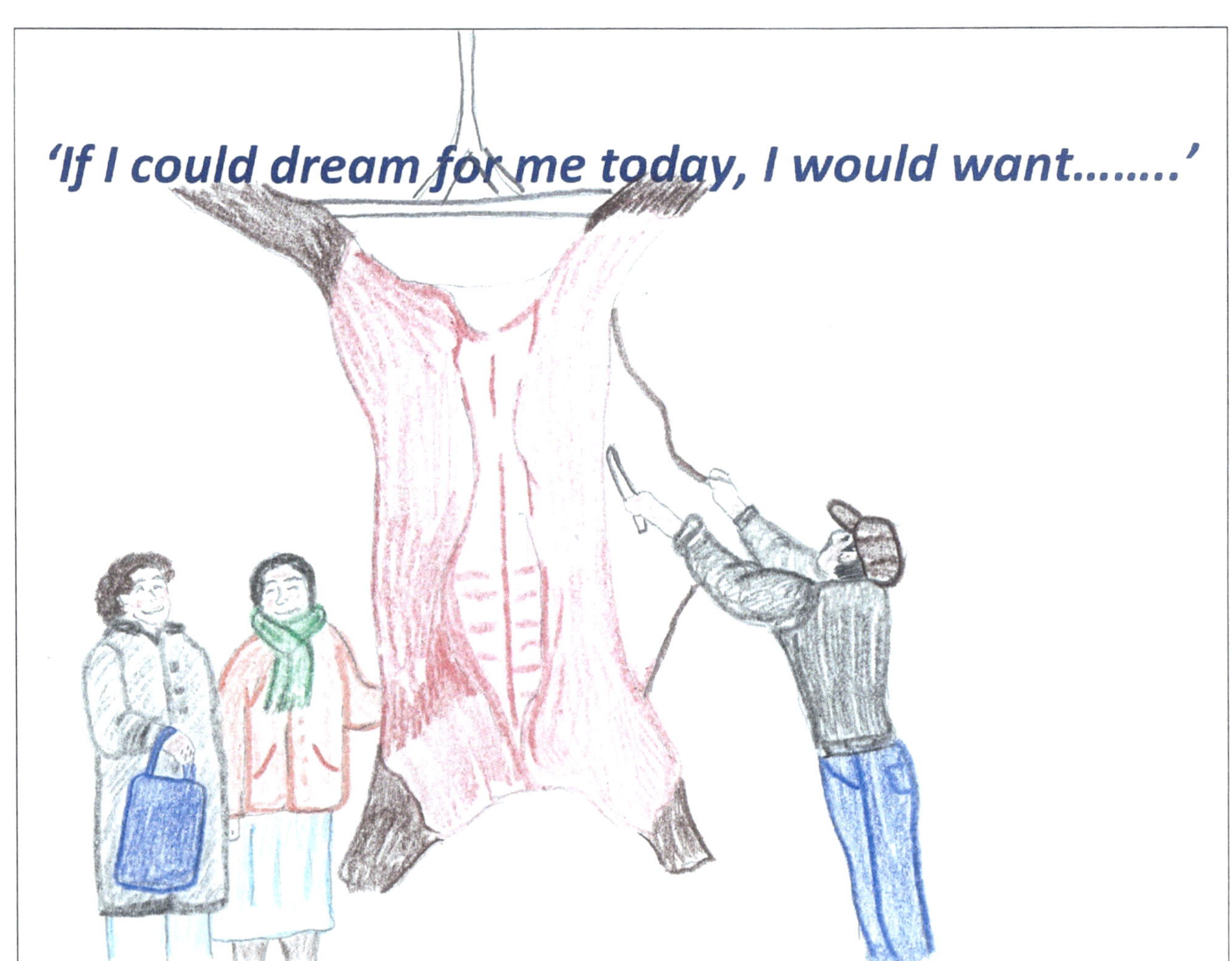

‘If I could dream for me today, I would want........’

People to bring back hunting

Matapiwa mahkaikskimahsa

'If I could dream for me today, I would want........'
Peigan
GOOD LEADERSHIP working with Community members
Council Chambers

That Chief & Council work with the people.

Miksi ninaiks mahkohpokapotakimahsi Piikani

That Chief & Council be intelligent

Miksi ninaiks mahkohkaokaksa

That Chief & Council be kind hearted

Miksi ninaiks mahkohkai kimapiyipitsa

Piikani Garden Market
'If I could dream for me today, I would want........'
Corn
Potatoes
Carrots

To work together as a Community

Ah kai to ma nis ta pot a koisi

'If I could dream for me today, I would want……..'

Travel the good road of health and strength

Mahk oht sapohs sokapiyi

Strong will

Sok sis tomsin, iyikitapisin

PiiKani Youth Centre..
'If I could dream for me today, I would want………'

To be a Youth Role model

Ahkits tsisi asitapi / pokaiks

Mahkayimatahsa

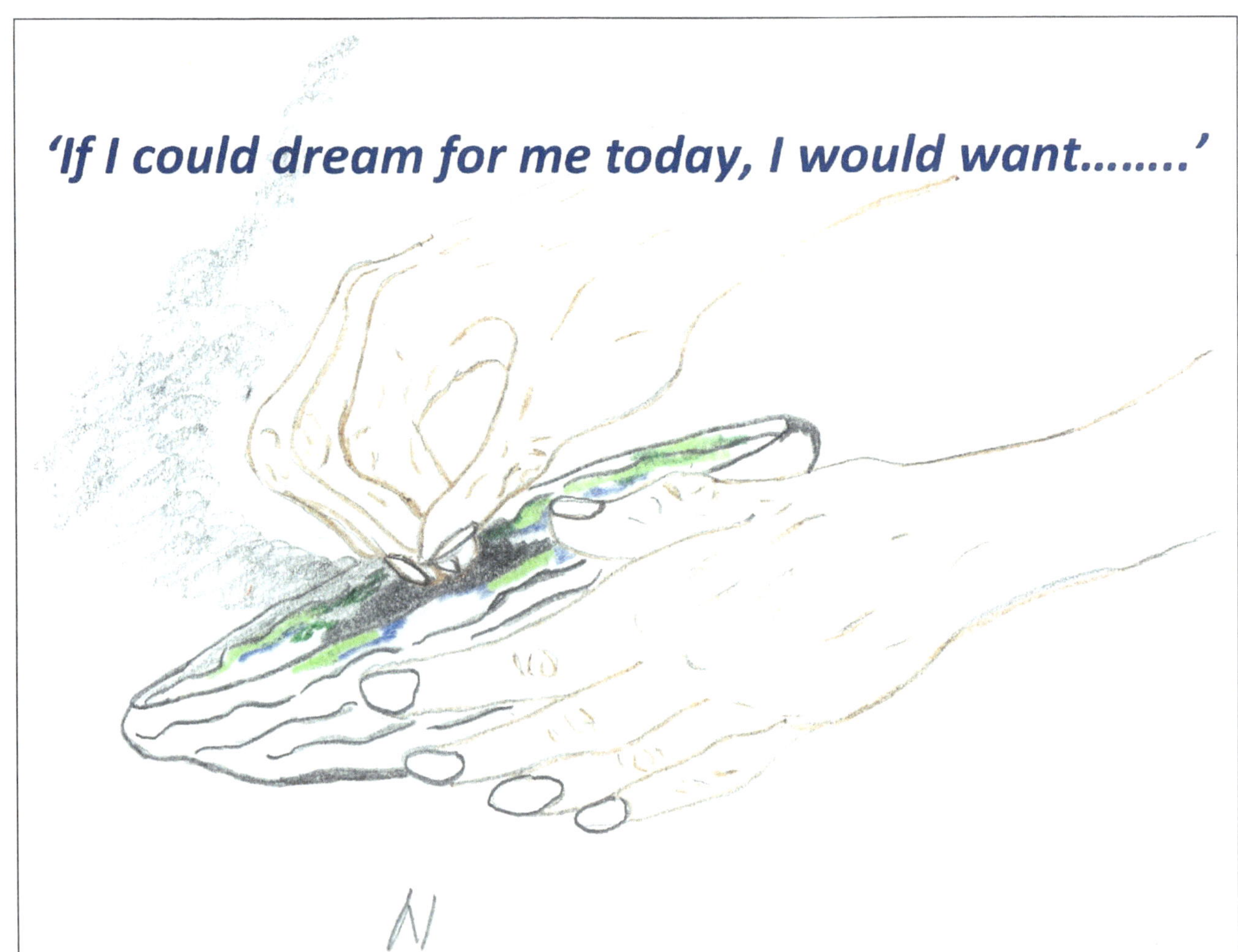

'If I could dream for me today, I would want........'

Use the real people ways

Nitsi tapia psin

'If I could dream for me today, I would want........'
Piikani working together to be drug free
Hwy #3

A drug free community- not to use- the people

Mahkitsawatohtoh koiskis matapiwa

What's used to feel high

Ihtais pimohsopi

'If I could dream for me today, I would want........'

Not for life to be easier, I should be stronger

Mahk sayik inapis patapisin Nahkohk
ayikakimahs

CREDITS

Lucille Provost
Author

A Piikani Nation member born and raised in Piikani. I am always looking for ways to support my people of the Piikani Nation.

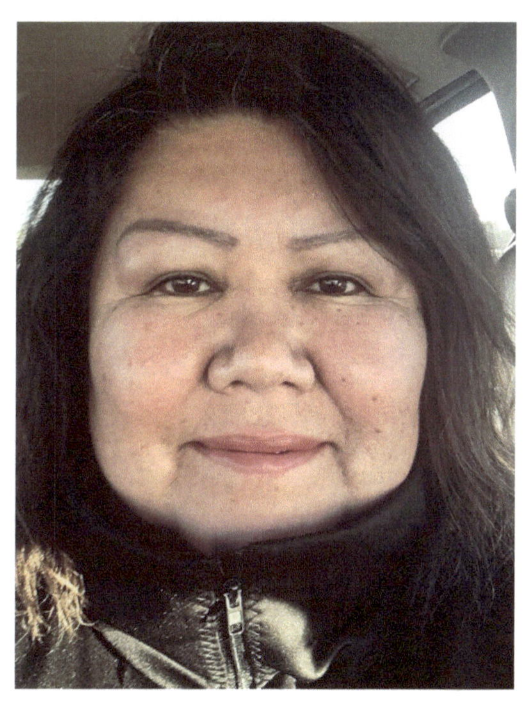

Dolly Yellow Wings
Illustrator

A Piikani Nation member born and raised in Piikani, always had a dream to illustrate Piikani Blackfoot books for our children and their families. It is a privilege to illustrate this book.

MORE FROM EAGLESPEAKER PUBLISHING

AUTHENTICALLY INDIGENOUS NAPI CHILDREN'S BOOKS:

Napi and the Rock

Napi and the Bullberries

Napi and the Wolves

Napi and the Buffalo

Napi and the Chickadees

Napi and the Coyote

Napi and the Elk

Napi and the Gophers

Napi and the Mice

Napi and the Prairie Chickens

Napi and the Bobcat

... and many more to come

AUTHENTICALLY INDIGENOUS GRAPHIC NOVELS:

UNeducation: A Residential School Graphic Novel

Napi the Trixster: A Blackfoot Graphic Novel

UNeducation, Vol 2

AUTHENTICALLY INDIGENOUS COLLABORATIONS:

The Great Cheyenne

Real Indian

Hello, Fruit Basket

... and countless more

AUTHENTICALLY INDIGENOUS KID'S BOOKS:

Teeias Goes to a Powwow

Please Don't Hide My Vegetables

www.eaglespeaker.com

**if you absolutely loved this book (or even just kind of liked it), please find it on Amazon.com and leave a quick review. Your words help more than you may realize.

www.ingramcontent.com/pod-product-compliance
Lightning Source LLC
Chambersburg PA
CBHW040140240726
48664CB00002B/553